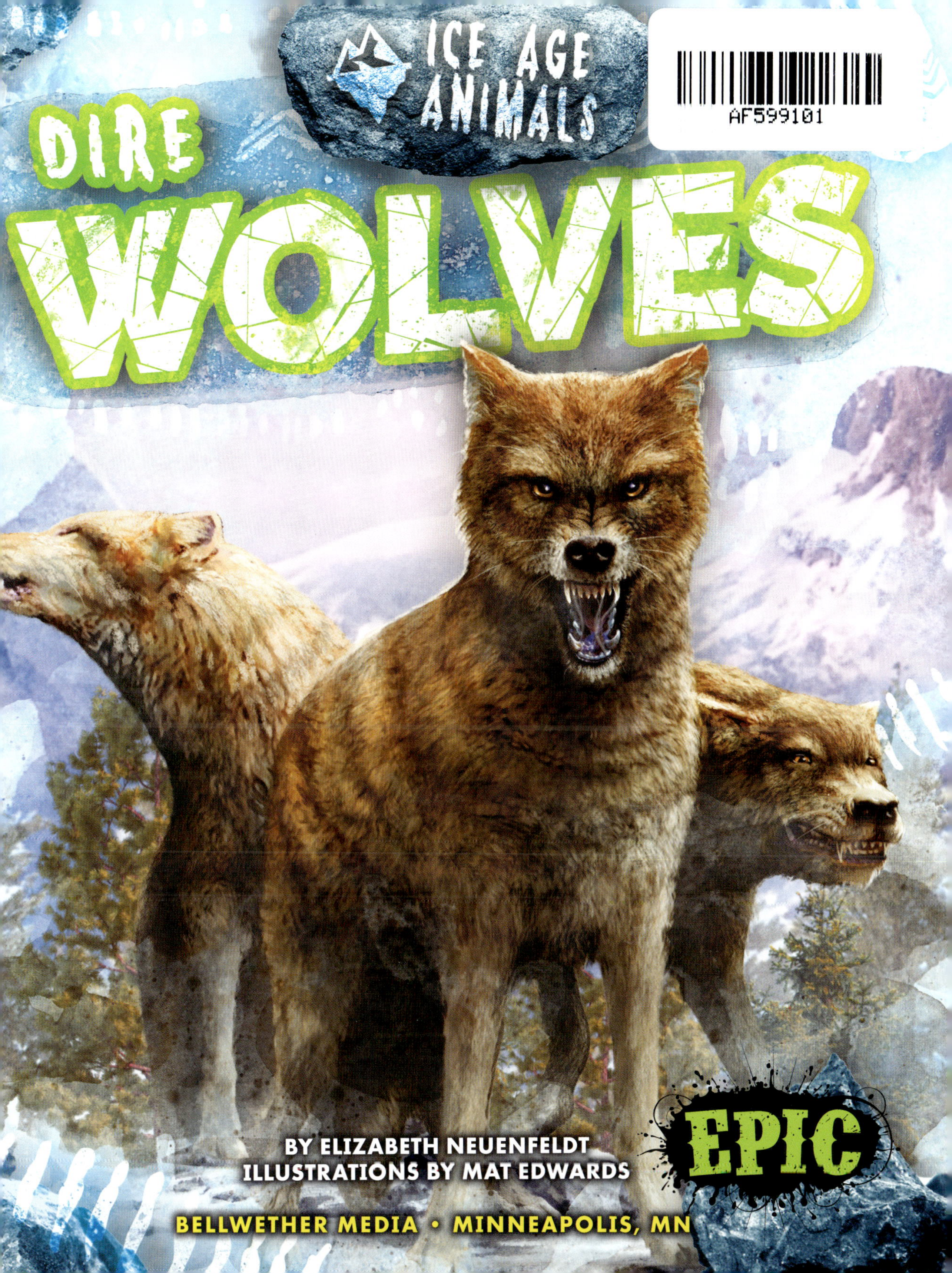
ICE AGE ANIMALS
DIRE
WOLVES
BY ELIZABETH NEUENFELDT
ILLUSTRATIONS BY MAT EDWARDS
BELLWETHER MEDIA • MINNEAPOLIS, MN
EPIC

This edition first published in 2025 by Bellwether Media, Inc.

Library of Congress Cataloging-in-Publication Data

Names: Neuenfeldt, Elizabeth, author.
Title: Dire wolves / by Elizabeth Neuenfeldt.
Description: Minneapolis, MN : Bellwether Media, Inc., 2025. | Series: Epic: Ice Age Animals | Includes bibliographical references and index. | Audience: Ages 7-12 | Audience: Grades 2-3 |
Summary: "Engaging images accompany information about dire wolves. The combination of high-interest subject matter and light text is intended for students in grades 2 through 7"-- Provided by publisher.
Identifiers: LCCN 2024019771 (print) | LCCN 2024019772 (ebook) | ISBN 9798893040401 (library binding) | ISBN 9798893041590 (paperback) | ISBN 9781644879801 (ebook)
Subjects: LCSH: Dire wolf--Juvenile literature. | Animals, Fossil--Juvenile literature.
Classification: LCC QE882.C15 .N474 2025 (print) | LCC QE882.C15 (ebook) | DDC 569/.77--dc23/eng/20240510
LC record available at https://lccn.loc.gov/2024019771
LC ebook record available at https://lccn.loc.gov/2024019772

Editor: Betsy Rathburn Designer: Jeffrey Kollock

Printed in the United States of America, North Mankato, MN.

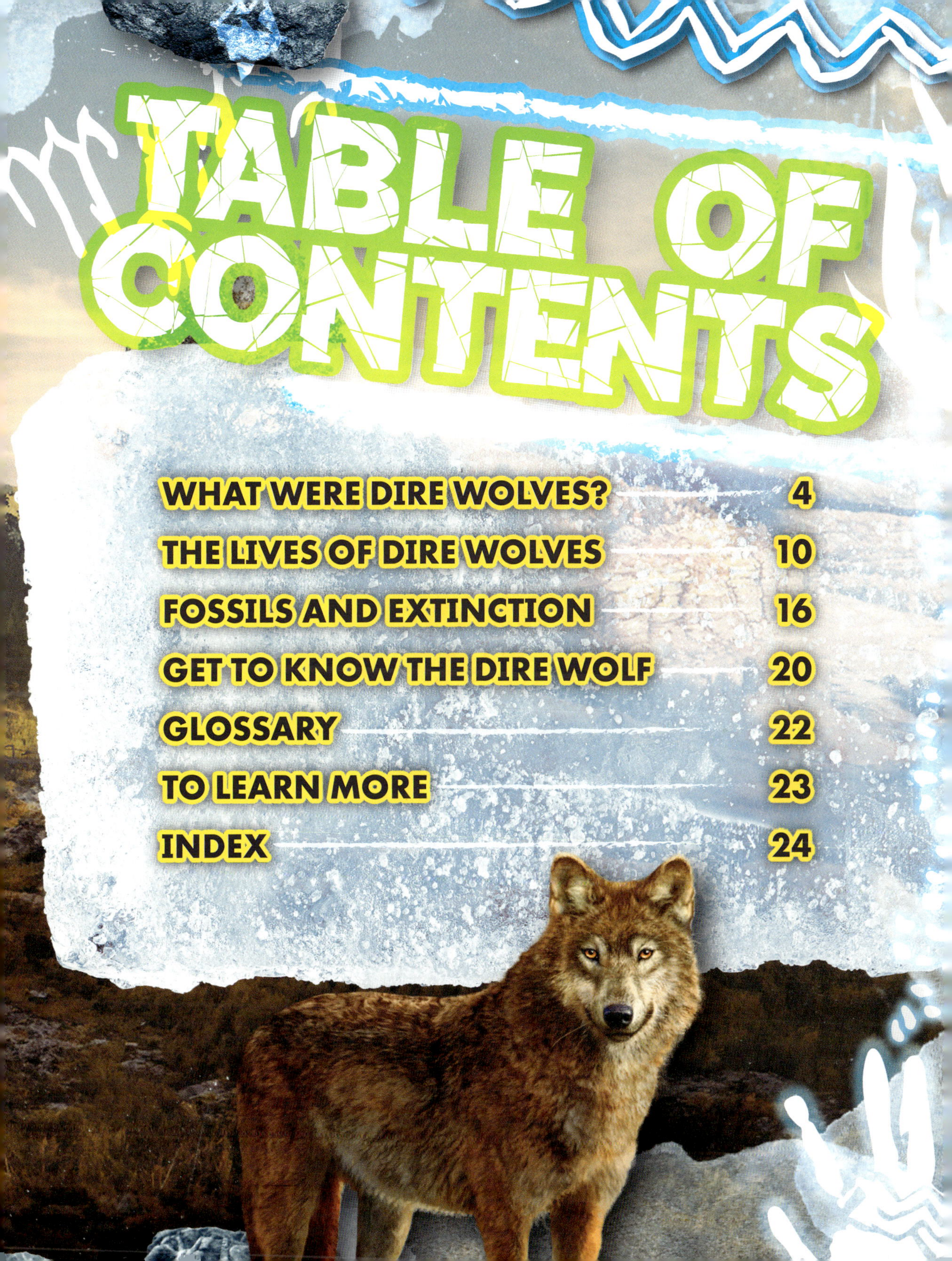

TABLE OF CONTENTS

WHAT WERE DIRE WOLVES?

ACROSS THE OCEAN

Dire wolf fossils were found in China in 2017. This shows they may have lived in Asia!

Dire wolves were top **predators**. They first lived around 250,000 years ago. This was during the **Pleistocene epoch**.

They mostly lived in North and South America.

Dire wolves had **stocky** bodies. They were very strong.

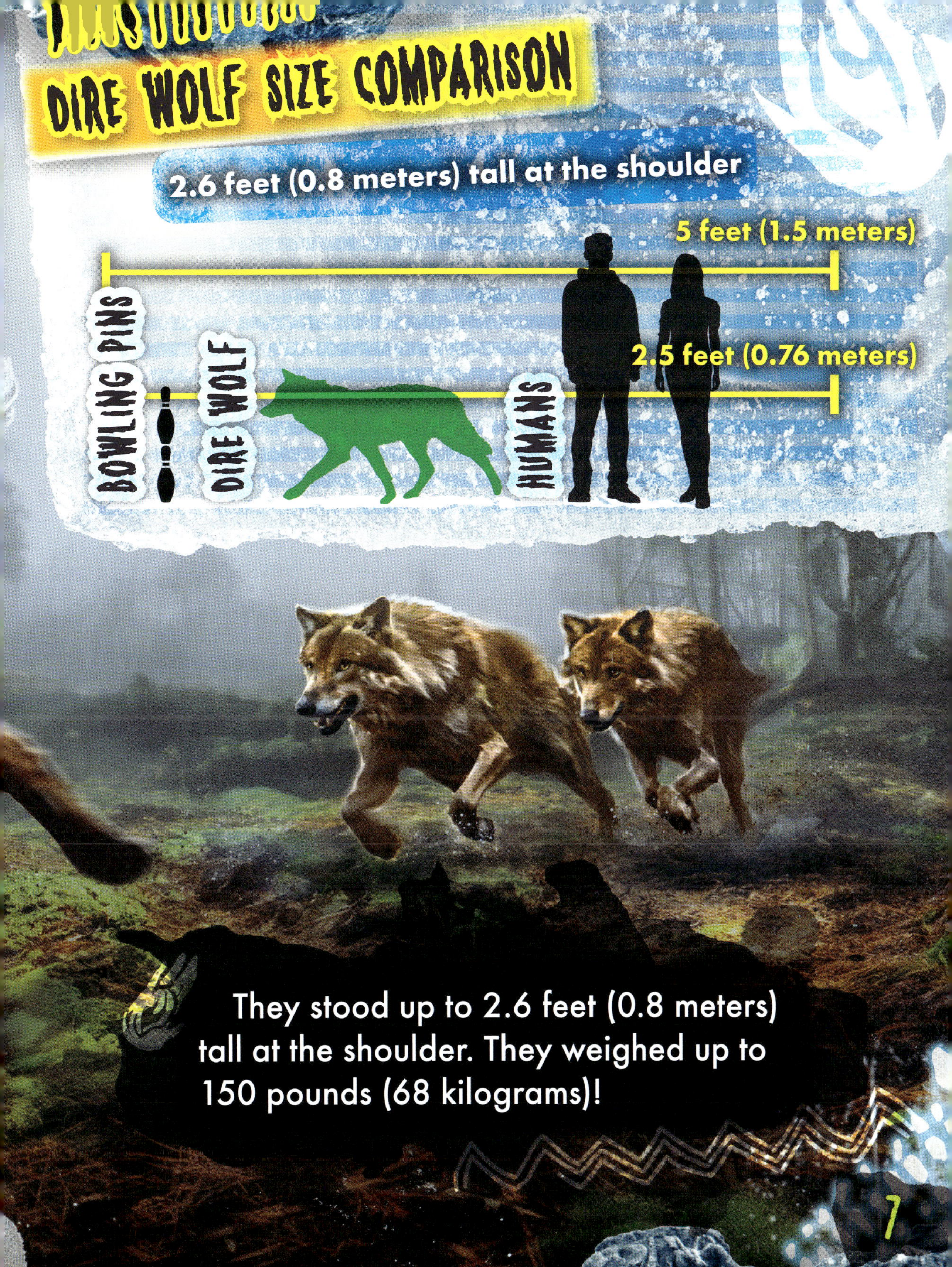

DIRE WOLF SIZE COMPARISON

They stood up to 2.6 feet (0.8 meters) tall at the shoulder. They weighed up to 150 pounds (68 kilograms)!

Dire wolves had reddish-brown fur. Their tails were long and bushy.

They had sharp teeth. They had strong jaws. They could bite through bones!
TWO-FOOT TAILS
Dire wolf tails were 2 feet (0.6 meters) long!
sharp teeth

THE LIVES OF DIRE WOLVES

Dire wolves were **carnivores**. They ate horses and bison. They also ate **carrion**.

They likely fought other animals for food. They may have fought early humans, too!

Dire wolves hunted in **packs**.
They could take down big animals.
prey

Dire wolf packs chased prey together. They attacked with their sharp teeth!
pack

Dire wolves were **mammals**. They may have formed **pair-bonds**. Females gave birth to live young.

Young dire wolves stayed with their packs. They learned how to hunt.

FOSSILS AND EXTINCTION

Dire wolves went **extinct** around 10,000 years ago. Humans overhunted their prey. Earth's changing **climate** killed prey, too. Dire wolves could not find food.

Many dire wolf **fossils** have been found. Most are from La Brea **Tar Pits**.

Dire wolves are related to today's jackals. Both animals are known for their reddish-brown fur and bushy tails.
DIRE WOLF
larger size
reddish-brown fur
bushy tail
lived mostly in North and South America

But jackals are smaller. They live in Africa. They help us learn more about dire wolves!

GET TO KNOW THE DIRE WOLF
powerful jaws
sharp teeth
WHEN WAS THE FIRST RECORDED FOSSIL FOUND?
1854 near Evansville, Indiana
stocky body
DIET
horses
bison
carrion

around 250,000 years ago
Dire wolves first appear

160,000 to 90,000 years ago
Early modern humans first appear

around 10,000 years ago
Dire wolves go extinct

reddish-brown fur

bushy tail

WEIGHT

up to 150 pounds (68 kilograms)

HEIGHT

up to 2.6 feet (0.8 meters) tall at the shoulder

WHERE DID THEY LIVE?

mostly in North and South America

GLOSSARY

carnivores—animals that only eat meat

carrion—the rotting meat of a dead animal

climate—the usual weather conditions in a particular place

extinct—no longer living

fossils—the remains of living things that lived long ago

mammals—warm-blooded animals that have backbones and feed their young milk

packs—groups of dire wolves that lived and hunted together

pair-bonds—close relationships between two animals that join together to make young

Pleistocene epoch—a time in history that lasted from around 2.58 million years ago to around 11,000 years ago and included the last ice age

predators—animals that hunt other animals for food

prey—animals that are hunted by other animals for food

stocky—having a solid, heavy body

tar pits—natural deposits of tar; tar is a dark, sticky liquid.

TO LEARN MORE

AT THE LIBRARY

Gish, Ashley. *Dire Wolves.* Mankato, Minn.: The Creative Company, 2023.

King, SJ. *The Secret Explorers and the Ice Age Adventure.* New York, N.Y.: DK Publishing, 2022.

Murray, Julie. *Dire Wolf.* Minneapolis, Minn.: ABDO, 2024.

ON THE WEB

FACTSURFER

Factsurfer.com gives you a safe, fun way to find more information.

1. Go to www.factsurfer.com.
2. Enter "dire wolves" into the search box and click 🔍.
3. Select your book cover to see a list of related content.

INDEX

The images in this book are reproduced through the courtesy of: Mat Edwards, front cover, pp. 4-5, 6-7, 8-9, 10-11, 12-13, 14-15, 16-17, 18-19, 20-21.